Shapes at home

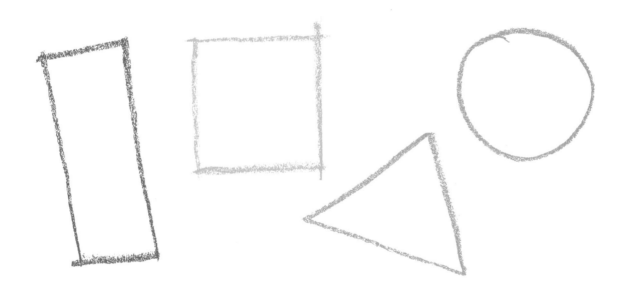

Lisa Bruce

Heinemann
LIBRARY

Little Nippers

H **www.heinemann.co.uk/library**
Visit our website to find out more information about **Heinemann Library** books.

To order:
☎ Phone 44 (0) 1865 888066
▤ Send a fax to 44 (0) 1865 314091
▢ Visit the Heinemann Bookshop at www.heinemann.co.uk/library to browse our catalogue and order online.

First published in Great Britain by Heinemann Library, Halley Court, Jordan Hill, Oxford OX2 8EJ, part of Harcourt Education.
Heinemann is a registered trademark of Harcourt Education Ltd.

Editorial: Jilly Attwood and Claire Throp
Design: Jo Hinton-Malivoire and bigtop, Bicester, UK
Models made by: Jo Brooker
Picture Research: Rosie Garai
Production: Séverine Ribierre

Originated by Dot Gradations
Printed and bound in China by South China Printing Company

ISBN 0 431 17191 2 (hardback)
07 06 05 04 03
10 9 8 7 6 5 4 3 2 1

ISBN 0 431 17196 3 (paperback)
07 06 05 04 03
10 9 8 7 6 5 4 3 2 1

British Library Cataloguing in Publication Data
Bruce, Lisa
Shapes at home – (Maths all around us)
516.1'5
A full catalogue record for this book is available from the British Library.

Acknowledgements
The Publishers would like to thank the following for permission to reproduce photographs: Argos p. **8**; Gareth Boden pp. **6–7, 11, 12, 15, 17, 18–19, 20–21, 22–23**; Pictures Colour Library p. **4**.

Cover photograph reproduced with permission of Gareth Boden.

The publishers would like to thank Annie Davy for her assistance in the preparation of this book.

Every effort has been made to contact copyright holders of any material reproduced in this book. Any omissions will be rectified in subsequent printings if notice is given to the publishers.

Contents

Squares

This is a square.

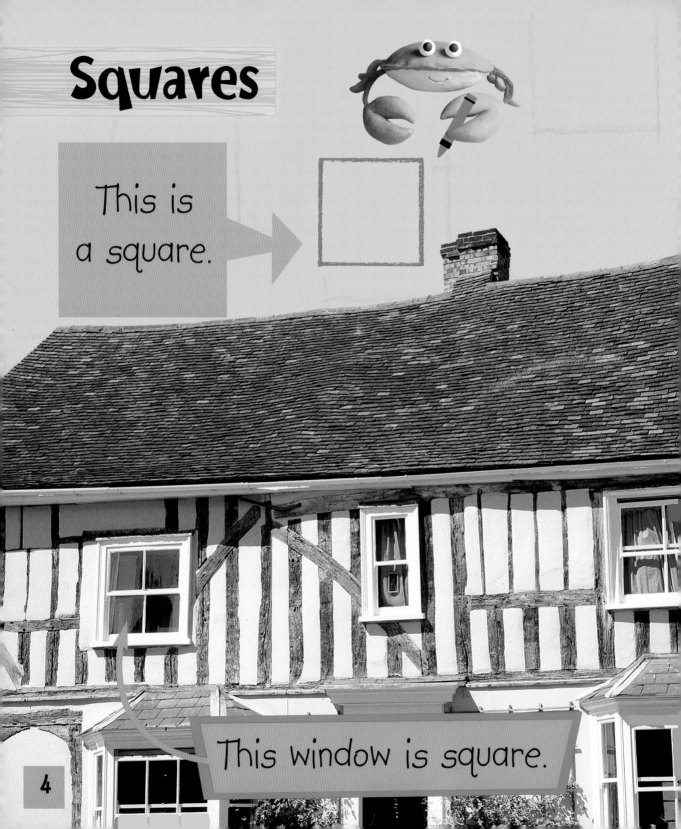

This window is square.

How many sides does a square have?

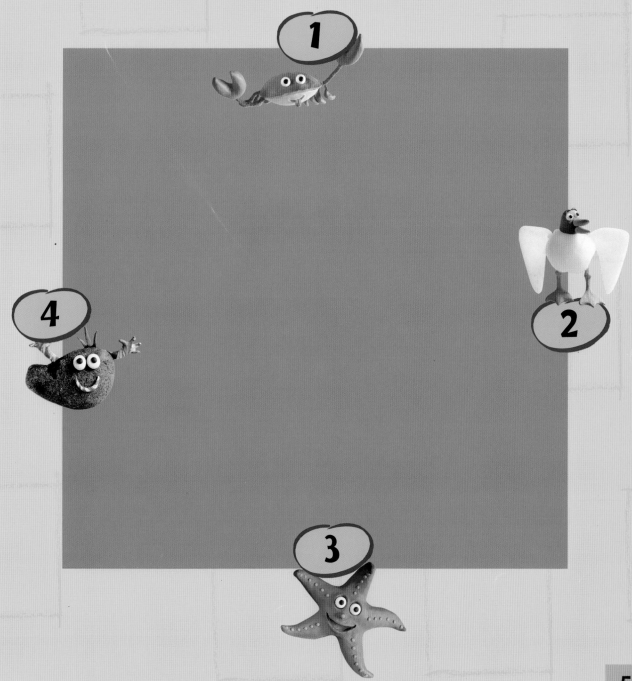

Can you find square shapes in the living room?

Rectangles

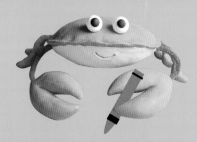

This is a
rectangle.

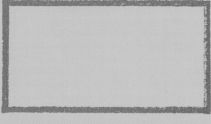

These drawers
are rectangles.

Two sides of a rectangle are long
and two sides are short.

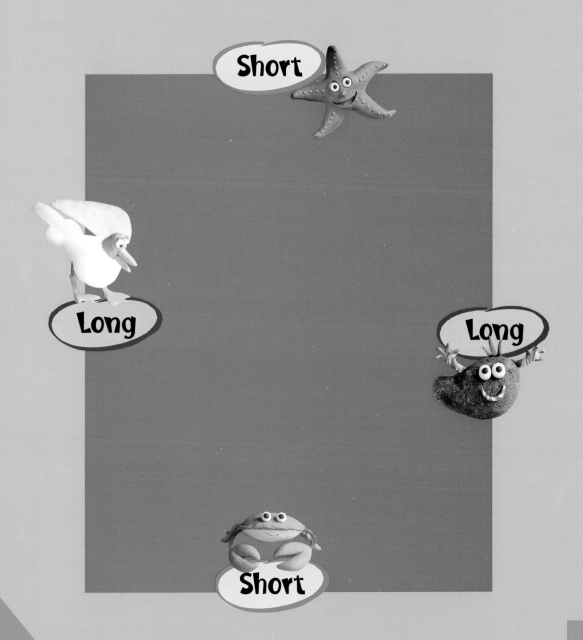

Rectangles in the house

There are lots of rectangles by the front door.

Can you see any rectangles in your house?

Circles

This is
a circle.

This
clock is
a circle.

12

Trace your finger around the outside of the circle. Is it straight or round?

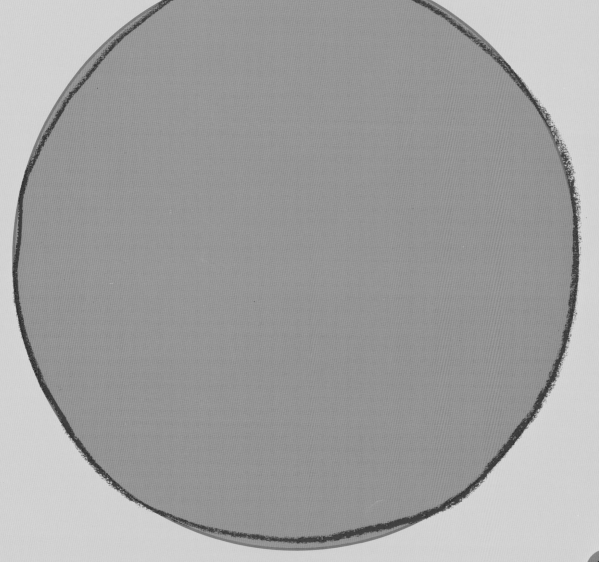

Circles in the house

Round and round
and round they go.

How many circles
do you know?

Triangles

A triangle has three sides.

This is a triangle.

3

1

2

How many points does a triangle have?

Triangles in the house

Yum!

What do you like to eat that is triangle shaped?

19

Other shapes

There are many other shapes that you can find in your home.

Oval egg

Crescent decoration

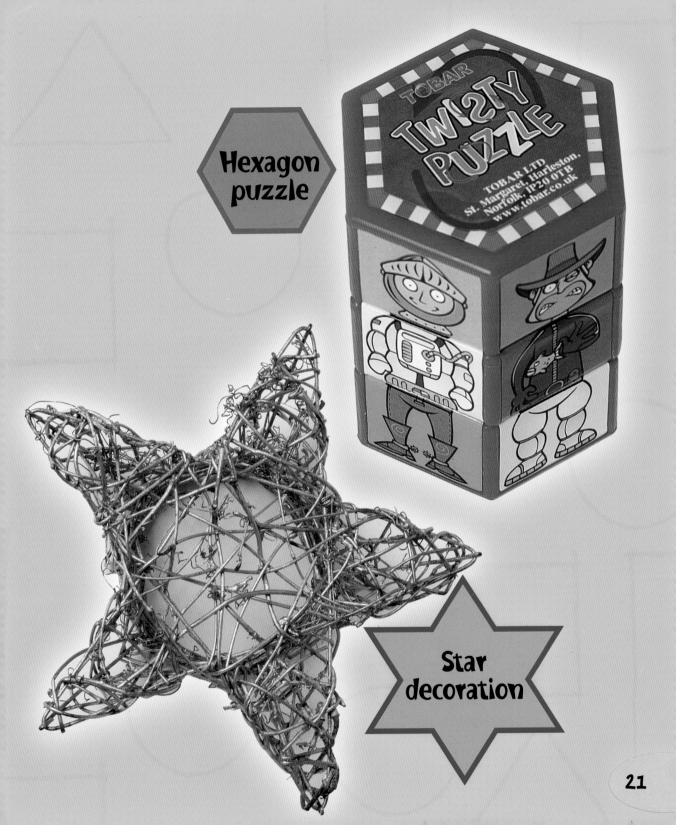

Hexagon puzzle

TOBAR
TWISTY PUZZLE
TOBAR LTD
St. Margaret, Harleston,
Norfolk, IP20 0TB
www.tobar.co.uk

Star decoration

Find the shape

What shapes can you find in the toy box?

Index

The end

Notes for adults

Maths all around us introduces children to basic mathematical concepts. The four books will help to form the foundation for later work in science and mathematics. The following Early Learning Goals are relevant to this series:
• say and use number names in order in familiar contexts
• count reliably up to 10 everyday objects
• recognise numerals 1 to 9
• use language, such as 'more' or 'less', to compare two numbers
• talk about, recognise and recreate simple patterns
• use language, such as 'circle' or 'bigger', to describe the shape and size of solids and flat shapes.

The *Maths all around us* series explores shapes, counting, patterns and sizes using familiar environments and objects to show children that there is maths all around us. The series will encourage children to think more about the structure of different objects around them and the relationships between them. It will also provide opportunities for discussing the importance of maths in a child's daily life. The series will encourage children to experience how different shapes feel, and to see how patterns can be made with shapes.

Shapes at home will help children extend their vocabulary, as they will hear new words such as *square, rectangle, trace, triangle, crescent, oval* and *hexagon*.

Follow-up activities
• Cut out various shapes from coloured paper and stick them on to a sheet to make a picture of: a house made of circles, a person made of triangles, a car made of squares, a tree made of rectangles. Ask the children if these are the best shapes to use for the pictures. Which shapes might be better?
• Cut card into rectangles and draw shapes on each card – squares, triangles, rectangles, stars. Use the cards to play Shapes Snap with the players having to identify the duplicate shapes before they can claim their prize.